DOWN THE PLUGHOLE!

The best way to read this book is to begin at the beginning and read all the way through.

You'll be amazed at what you'll find out.

But if you want to read about one particular thing, such as toilets or dandruff, look in the index on page 33.

Thompson Yardley wrote this book and drew the pictures. He has done a lot of other things as well as writing books such as repairing furniture and driving lorries.

ISBN 0 304 31776 4

First published in 1990 by
Cassell Publishers Limited
Artillery House, Artillery Row
London SW1P 1RT

© Copyright 1990 Lazy Summer Books Limited

Printed and bound in Great Britain
by MacLehose & Partners Ltd, Portsmouth

HAVE YOU HAD
A BATH
TODAY?

DON'T JUST DIVE IN!..

FIND OUT...why you have to wash!

FIND OUT...what to do if your toe gets stuck in the tap!

FIND OUT...where loofahs come from!

FIND OUT...how to make GIANT BUBBLES!

What would it be like if you

NEVER WASHED?

Would the dirt build up on your skin so that after about 20 years you would look like this?...

SKIN SHEDDING FACT

Your skin never stops growing. The outer layer keeps peeling off and takes the dirt with it.

NO! But you might smell a bit! That's because very small creatures called bacteria live on skin and in dirt.

These are usually called germs.

They can give off horrible smelly gases.

Dead skin peels off in flakes that are sometimes too small to see

BACTERIA GAS FACT

Bacteria in your intestines can produce a litre of gas each day!

BACTERIA

As well as bad smells, bacteria sometimes cause illnesses such as...

TETANUS! **CHOLERA!**

FOOD POISONING!

TYPHOID! **DYSENTERY!**

Most of these illnesses are caused by drinking dirty water.

Because these harmful bacteria live in dirt, you have to wash off the dirt to get rid of most of them.

But they soon come back...

BACTERIA BABY-BOOM FACT

Bacteria grow very quickly. They can double their number every twenty minutes.

1. A single bacteria is called a bacterium.

Here's one bacterium left after washing.

2. After twenty minutes,

it splits into two bacteria.

BACTERIA BRAIN BAFFLER

If these bacteria carry on growing like this, how many will there be after four hours?

3. After forty minutes,

they split into four bacteria.

4. After one hour,

they split into eight bacteria, and so on.

*Answer to **BACTERIA BRAIN BAFFLER:***
Four thousand and ninety-six

SOAP AND SKIN

Here's a common sort of bacteria...

They are so small that you could get more than a thousand into the space taken up by this full stop.

The ones above are called **STREPTOCOCCI.** They live in your intestines. If you don't wash your hands after using the toilet, streptococci can get into your mouth. Then you may get a sore throat.

Soap makes washing easier. But...not all types of soap get rid of all types of bacteria. Some bacteria will still be alive even if your skin looks spotless.

But...don't worry, your body can fight small numbers of bacteria. It's only if there are too many that you become ill.

BLEACH DANGER FACT

Some chemical cleaners such as bleach have a sign to say that they are poisonous or one to show that they are corrosive. Corrosive means that it damages your skin and other surfaces.

POISON   CORROSIVE

SOAP AND SKIN

Skin is the largest organ of the body. It keeps your insides in and the outside out!

People who scrub their hands too hard can damage the skin and get a rash. This is because the skin is protected by a thin film of oil which is easily washed off. Harmless bacteria living in the oil protect the skin from more harmful bacteria.

But...soap can kill both sorts! So washing can help harmful bacteria to invade your body.

Pumice stone is a rough sort of rock found near volcanoes. It's used to scrub away stains on the skin. But...it can damage the skin, letting harmful bacteria in.

SKIN

Here's a close-up of a bit of skin.

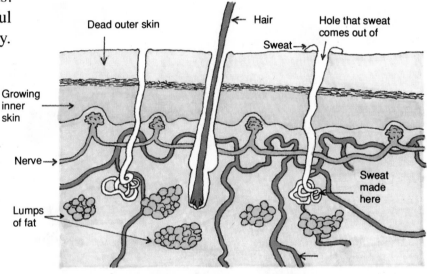

Dead outer skin
Hair
Hole that sweat comes out of
Sweat
Growing inner skin
Nerve →
Sweat made here
Lumps of fat

Soap loosens dirt from the skin. It also washes away some of the dead skin, taking the dirt away with it. Notice how your fingertips feel smoother after washing...

Close-up of fingerprints before washing:

Enlarged side view of skin

Close-up of fingerprints after washing:

Side view

5

HAIR

SHAMPOO

Until recently, people brushed their hair to keep it clean. This made it glossy and strong. These days people usually wash their hair in shampoo. This is quicker but too much washing removes natural oils and can damage the hair. You don't need to wash your hair every day.

Dandruff isn't dirt, it's just flakes of skin from your scalp.

A BAD CASE OF DANDRUFF

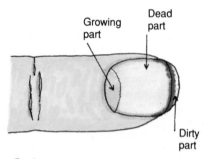

Growing part · Dead part · Dirty part

Only part of a fingernail is growing. The end which you cut off is dead. That's why it doesn't hurt when you trim them. The dead part is pushed out by the growing part.

The best way to clean dirty fingernails is with a stiff nail-brush.

FINGERNAILS

Fingernails are great places for bacteria to live. You can spread bacteria all over your body whe you scratch!

SCRITCH!

SCRATCH!

WRIGGLE!

TEETH

Have you brushed your teeth today?

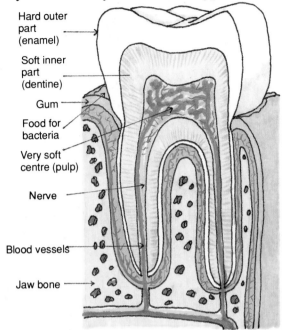

Hard outer part (enamel)

Soft inner part (dentine)

Gum

Food for bacteria

Very soft centre (pulp)

Nerve

Blood vessels

Jaw bone

CLOSE-UP OF A TOOTH

Bad teeth are caused by tiny bacteria. They live on bits of food left on your teeth after eating. These bacteria give off acids which make holes in the hard surface of the teeth. Then the softer inner part soon rots away.
Bacteria grow quickly on sugary sticky food such as biscuits and sweets.

Yum! Yum!

Mm!

It's a good idea to clean your teeth after every meal as well as before going to bed. Brush your teeth the way your dentist shows you. Brushing properly is much more important than the type of toothpaste you use.

Older children and adults should have thirty-two teeth. Ask your parents how many bad teeth they've had taken out. You may be surprised!

TOOTHPASTE UNFAIR TO TOOTH FAIRIES!

Of course, if you're dirty all over, you'll need a bath or a shower...

SHOWER POWER...

There are lots of different showers too!
Here's the sort that people use in baths.

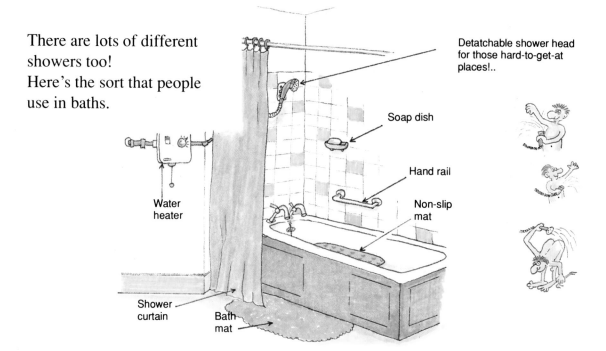

Detatchable shower head for those hard-to-get-at places!..

Soap dish

Hand rail

Non-slip mat

Water heater

Shower curtain

Bath mat

SHOWERS OR BATHS

Showers are much more hygienic than baths. When you take a bath, the dirt stays in the water with you.

Soaking in the bath feels great, but showers use a lot less water.

TRY IT OUT!..

1. Plug the outlet hole with some soap. Take a shower and see how much water you've used. Don't let the water overflow!

2. Compare it with the amount of water you need for a bath.

TRY THIS SHOWERY TONGUE - TWISTER!
SLIPPY SOAPY STEAMY SHOWERS CERTAINLY SAVE SOAKING SKIN IN SUDS!

ERK!

TO THE DOCTOR

Have you ever wondered why putting water in a bath is called...

RUNNING A BATH?..

FINISH

Baths are shaped so that an adult can relax like this...

BUT... baths are too short to lie down in, so there's less chance of slipping under the water and drowning. Young people aren't so tall, so try not to doze off! Check the temperature before you get in a hot bath!..

Feet touch bottom end

Head rests on top end

Plughole

The bath slopes so that the water can run out down the plughole

YOW!

PLUGHOLE SUCTION FACT

Don't put your hands or any other part of your body near the plughole when the water's running out. Water going down the hole makes a strong sucking force which can break your wrist!

WHAT TO DO IF YOU SCALD YOURSELF

Hold the scalded part under cold running water for a while. Keep it there until it stops hurting. Don't put creams or soap or antiseptic on the scald. They can stop your skin from healing properly.
If it's a really bad scald or burn, see a doctor.

TRY THIS AND SEE!..
1. Pull out the plug and let the water run out.
2. Dangle the plug over the hole and feel the suction of the water as it tries to pull the plug down the hole.

GLUG!

SINKS and PLUGS

Here's a common sort of sink...

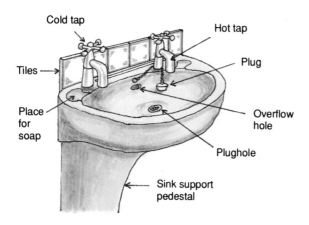

The overflow hole is there in case you leave the plug in the plughole and the tap running.

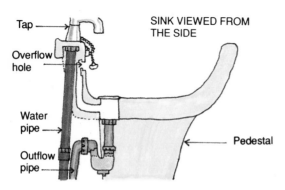

When the water-level reaches the hole, water pours down the channel at the back of the sink to the outflow pipe. This stops you from flooding the bathroom.

Here's a plug and plughole...

Plugholes are shaped the way they are so that small objects like rings can't be sucked down them.

Two ways water can swirl

Water doesn't fall down the hole. It swirls round first. But...which way round does it go in your sink?

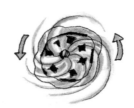

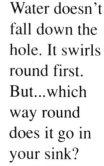

Check it out! Fill the sink and float a small piece of toilet paper. Pull out the plug and see which way round the paper goes.
Can you make the water swirl the other way round? Try stirring it before you pull out the plug!

TAPS

There are lots of different taps.

Push-top tap

Glass-topped tap

Mixer tap

Another mixer tap

Tap for disabled people

Old-fashioned tap

Taps work like this...

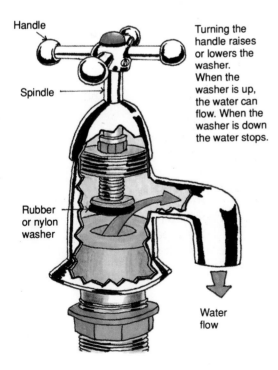

Handle

Spindle

Rubber or nylon washer

Turning the handle raises or lowers the washer. When the washer is up, the water can flow. When the washer is down the water stops.

Water flow

WHAT TO DO IF YOUR TOE GETS STUCK!..

Yow!

1. If it's the cold tap, turn it on and the force of the water might push your toe out!

2. If it's the hot tap, don't turn it on, you'll scald yourself! Get some soap and squeeze a bit up into the tap. It should come out!

3. If it's still stuck... shout for help!

Help!

A shower-head is a bit like a long tap except that it has lots of small holes instead of one large one. The water shoots out of the small holes with more power than from an ordinary tap.

TRY THIS

1. Fill an old washing-up liquid bottle with water.
2. Squirt it with the lid on and see how far the water goes.
3. Now squirt it with the lid off.

SSSS!

FLOB!

All of the pipes in a house are called the

PLUMBING

BUT...it's got nothing to do with plums! The name comes from an old word for lead.

The house-pipes carry water to all the taps in the house.

These pipes are connected to the main pipe which brings water to the house.

Outside most houses, there's an underground tap. This is used to cut off the supply of water to the house.
If a plumber has to repair any water-pipes, the water supply has to be cut off first!

This plumber forgot!

WATER METER FACT
In some countries, the amount of water supplied to a house is measured by a meter. People pay for the amount they use. This encourages them not to waste it.

BONK!

**BATHS
£1 EACH**

How much would **you** pay for a bath?

WHAT'S WATER WORTH?

Think what it would be like if you were lost in a hot desert with no water...

You'd be thirsty!..

How much money would you give for a glass of water?

All your pocket money? Or more?

If you were dying of thirst, you'd think a glass of water was worth all the money in the world!

Poor people who live in hot, dry countries often have to walk a long way to get water. That's because they can't afford to build pipes to bring it to them.

CLEAN WATER FACT

It costs a lot to make sure water is clean. There are five billion people in the world. Of these, three and a half billion can't afford clean water to drink and clean toilets to use.

Clean drinking water is valuable, so try not to waste it. Next time you use the bathroom, remember how much water is worth!

BATHROOM BITS AND BOBS

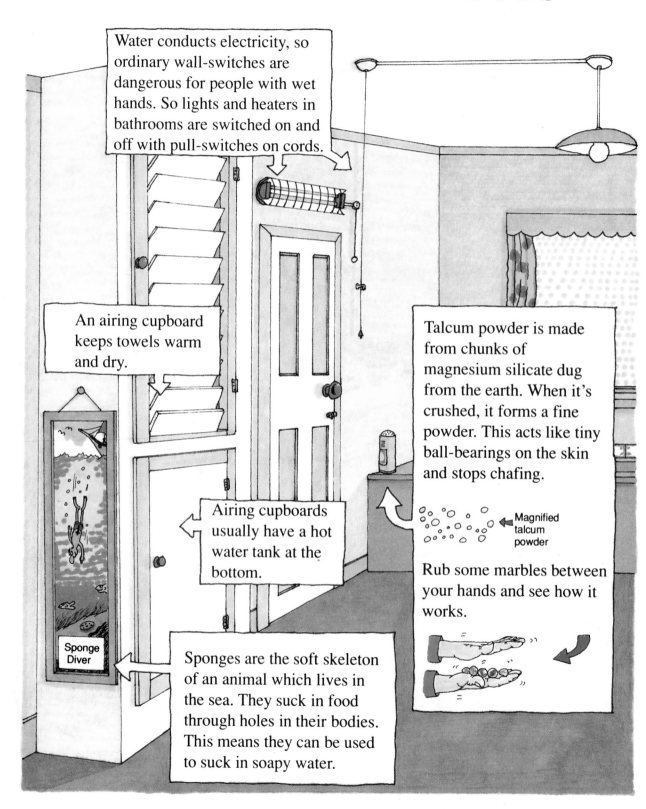

Water conducts electricity, so ordinary wall-switches are dangerous for people with wet hands. So lights and heaters in bathrooms are switched on and off with pull-switches on cords.

An airing cupboard keeps towels warm and dry.

Airing cupboards usually have a hot water tank at the bottom.

Sponge Diver

Sponges are the soft skeleton of an animal which lives in the sea. They suck in food through holes in their bodies. This means they can be used to suck in soapy water.

Talcum powder is made from chunks of magnesium silicate dug from the earth. When it's crushed, it forms a fine powder. This acts like tiny ball-bearings on the skin and stops chafing.

← Magnified talcum powder

Rub some marbles between your hands and see how it works.

BATHROOM BITS AND BOBS

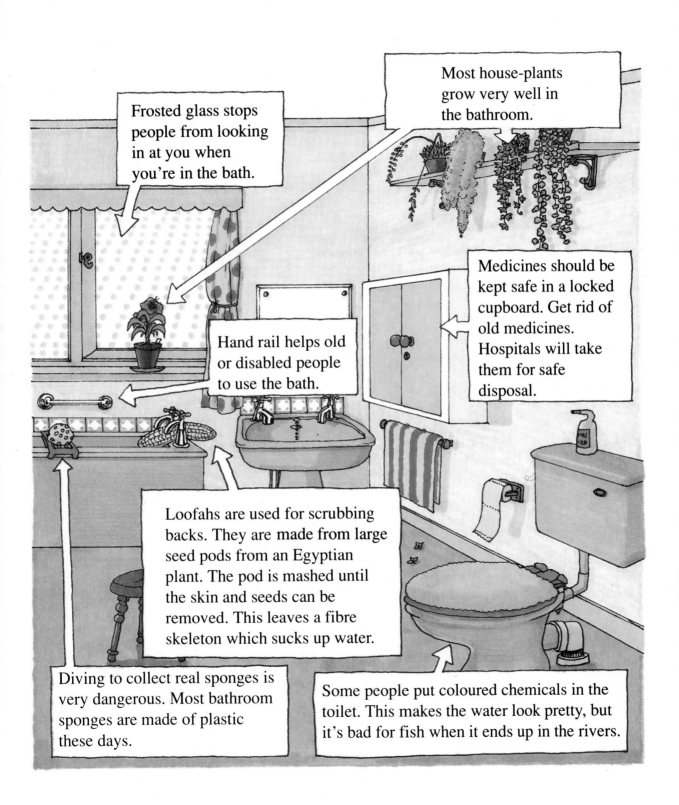

Frosted glass stops people from looking in at you when you're in the bath.

Most house-plants grow very well in the bathroom.

Medicines should be kept safe in a locked cupboard. Get rid of old medicines. Hospitals will take them for safe disposal.

Hand rail helps old or disabled people to use the bath.

Loofahs are used for scrubbing backs. They are made from large seed pods from an Egyptian plant. The pod is mashed until the skin and seeds can be removed. This leaves a fibre skeleton which sucks up water.

Diving to collect real sponges is very dangerous. Most bathroom sponges are made of plastic these days.

Some people put coloured chemicals in the toilet. This makes the water look pretty, but it's bad for fish when it ends up in the rivers.

TOILET TROUBLES

Everybody has to use the toilet, but lots of people think we shouldn't talk about them.

There are lots of names for toilets...

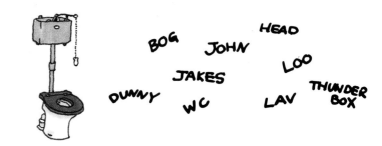

Can you think of any more?!

Bacteria live well in toilets. They like damp places. After you've used the toilet, your hands can spread bacteria to...

THE PAPER

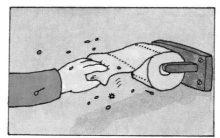

THE SEAT

THE TOILET HANDLE

THE LIGHT SWITCH

THE DOOR HANDLE

Everyone who uses the toilet can spread bacteria.

SO...if you don't wash, you'll spread bacteria all over the house!

HOW TO STOP THE SPREAD OF BACTERIA

1. Always make sure there's enough toilet paper first!
2. Try not to miss!
3. Flush the bowl afterwards!
4. Wash your hands!

TOILET TROUBLES

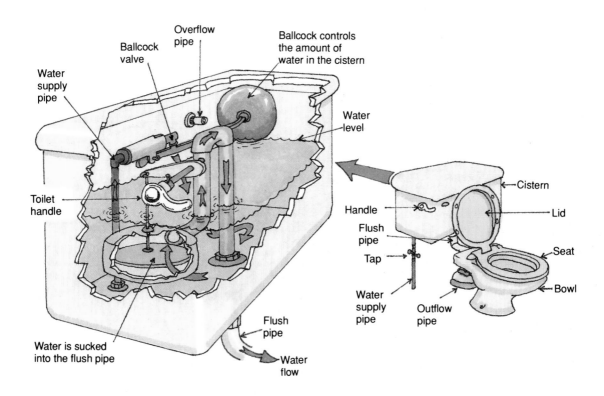

Overflow pipe

Ballcock valve

Ballcock controls the amount of water in the cistern

Water supply pipe

Water level

Water supply pipe

Toilet handle

Cistern

Handle

Lid

Flush pipe

Tap

Seat

Bowl

Water is sucked into the flush pipe

Water supply pipe

Outflow pipe

Flush pipe

Water flow

HOW TO UNBLOCK A TOILET

Toilets sometimes become blocked up.
Here are two ways to unblock them.

1. Pour a bucket of water quickly down the bowl. This will often force the blockage down the hole.

SLOOOSH!

2. If the first method doesn't work, get a plunger which looks like this.

Ram the plunger up and down in the hole at the bottom of the bowl. It makes a great noise as well as clearing the blockage.

SCHLOOP!

SLURP!

BLUNGE!

What would it be like if you flushed yourself...

DOWN THE TOILET??..

The bend is full of water to stop smells from coming back up the pipe.

1. FIRST..
You'd go round the bend!..

2. Then you'd go down the toilet outflow pipe...

3. Then you'd get washed out into the sewer pipe under the road outside.
Here, you'd join the waste from other people's houses...
and it smells terrible.

4. The small sewer pipe joins the main sewer pipe. These can be big enough to drive a car down! All the grates in your street let rain water into the sewer pipes.

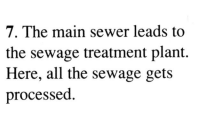

5. Main sewers often have walkways so that workmen can walk along them and check the condition of the walls and floors.

6. Sometimes, there are dry parts where rats live. In some American cities there have been reports of alligators living in the sewers!..

7. The main sewer leads to the sewage treatment plant. Here, all the sewage gets processed.

8. Finally, you'd be washed up against a grating where all the large solids are trapped. These solids are fished out every so often, so you'd be rescued at last!

At certain times of the day, too much waste can flow into the sewage plant. Then it has to be pumped straight into a river or the sea. This causes pollution.

It would be better if people used water at different times of the day. This would spread out water use so that the sewage plants aren't overloaded.

Why not find out about water use in your house? You'll be surprised at how much water a household uses during a single day!

MAKE A WATER-WATCHER'S WALLCHART

WATER-WATCHER'S WALLCHART

LITRES USED	WHEN	BY WHOM	PURPOSE
1	0.815	DAD	POT OF TEA
7	0820	MUM	WASHING HANDS
7	08.22	DAD	WASHING CUPS
10	08.30	DARREN	TOILET
8	08.35	TRACEY	SHOWER
½	08.50	MUM	WATERING PLANTS
¼	08.53	TRACEY	WATER FOR CAT
½	08.55	DARREN	WATER PISTOL

1. Find out how much water is used in...

a washing machine
a bath
a toilet
a washing-up bowl.

2. Make yourself a chart like this.

3. When somebody in your house uses some water, enter the details into the chart.

4. Before you go to bed, add up how much water has been used.

9. Sewage is full of bacteria, some of which can make you ill. You'd have to go to hospital to find out if you'd caught any diseases.

That means you'd miss...

WHAT HAPPENS NEXT...

Here's a simplified plan of a sewage treatment station. Sewage is made up of liquid and sludge. They are split up and the treated liquid is pumped into the river. The dried sludge is used as fertilizer

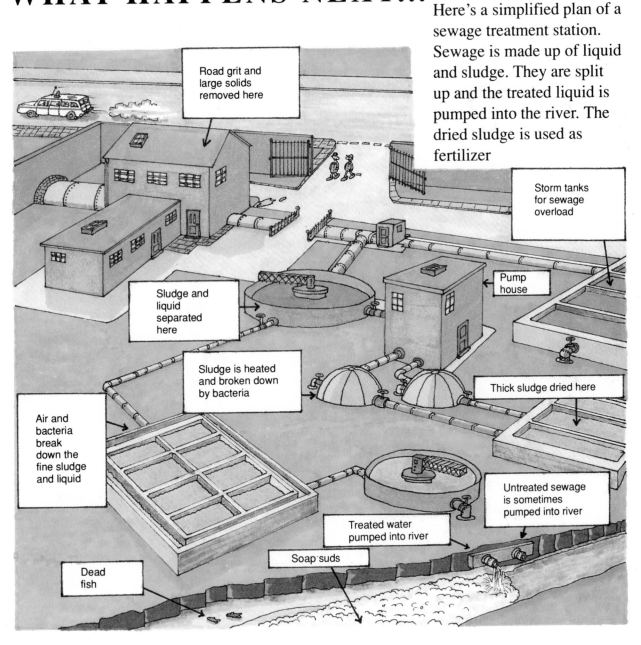

Road grit and large solids removed here

Storm tanks for sewage overload

Pump house

Sludge and liquid separated here

Sludge is heated and broken down by bacteria

Thick sludge dried here

Air and bacteria break down the fine sludge and liquid

Untreated sewage is sometimes pumped into river

Treated water pumped into river

Soap suds

Dead fish

WATER SUPPLY

Most of our water supply comes from rivers.
BUT... rivers can become very polluted by waste from factories and farms.
So... rivers are dammed before they reach the polluted areas. The water collects above the dam in man-made lakes called reservoirs.

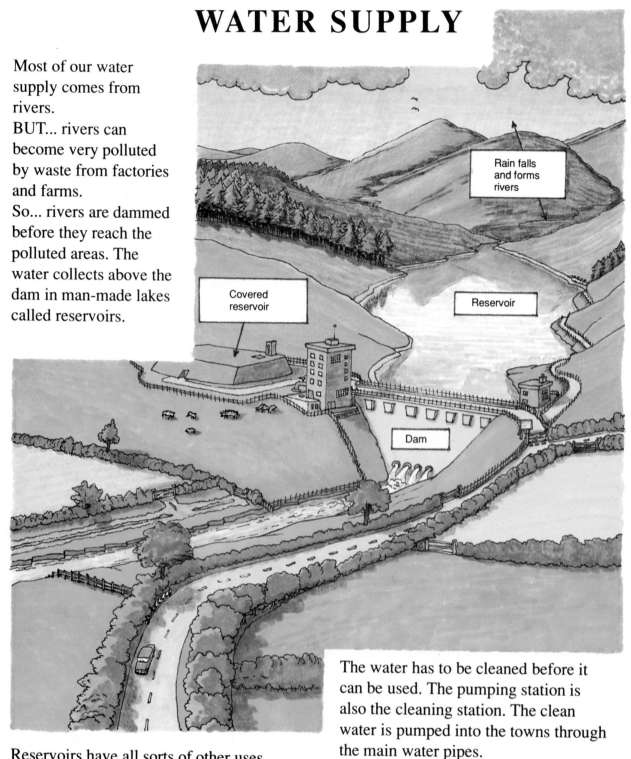

Rain falls and forms rivers

Covered reservoir

Reservoir

Dam

Reservoirs have all sorts of other uses too. Sailing, fishing and water skiing for example.

The water has to be cleaned before it can be used. The pumping station is also the cleaning station. The clean water is pumped into the towns through the main water pipes.
Sometimes the water is pumped to covered reservoirs where it is stored for later use.

22

UNDERGROUND RIVERS

Rivers can run underground too!
Sometimes wells are bored to pump
the water to the surface.

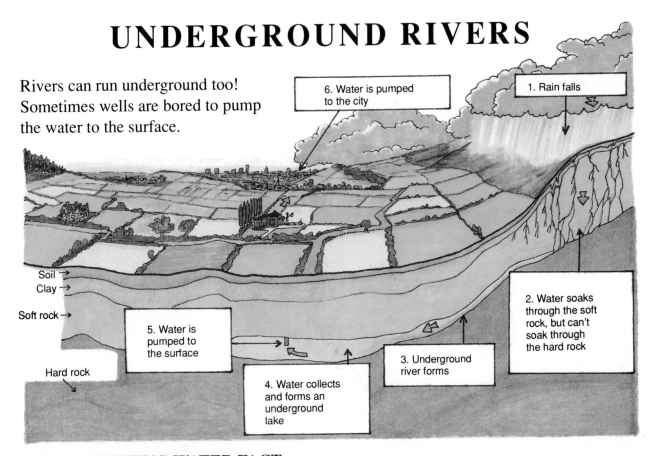

6. Water is pumped to the city

1. Rain falls

Soil
Clay

Soft rock

5. Water is pumped to the surface

Hard rock

2. Water soaks through the soft rock, but can't soak through the hard rock

3. Underground river forms

4. Water collects and forms an underground lake

WELL-WISHING WATER FACT

Hundreds of years ago, people thought
that there were water gods living in
wells. They had to pay these gods so
that the well didn't dry up. That's why
people still throw coins into wells and
make a wish!

I wish I hadn't thrown my bus fare down there!

Underground rivers are usually much
cleaner than surface rivers. That means
it's worthwhile digging wells or
bore-holes to get the water.

Most rivers finish up in the sea.

SAD SEA-WATER FACT

Most of the Earth's surface is covered
by the sea. There's enough water in the
world to make all the deserts fertile.
BUT... sea water is too salty to use, and
it costs too much to take the salt out.
Only one litre out of every thousand we
use comes from purified sea water.

MAIN WATER PIPES

In most towns, main water pipes are laid under roads. This is because it's fairly easy to dig a hole in the road when a pipe needs to be repaired.
BUT...being under the road means that they can be damaged by traffic such as heavy lorries and buses.

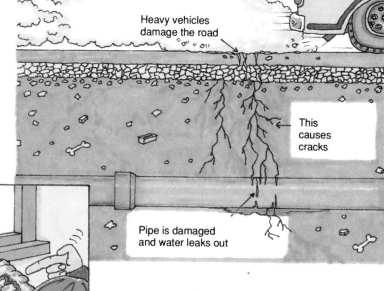

Heavy vehicles damage the road

This causes cracks

Pipe is damaged and water leaks out

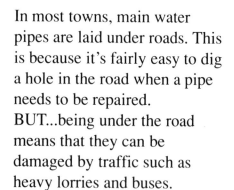

Water companies keep maps which show where the pipes are. Some of the maps are very old!

BUT...many pipes have been in the ground for so long that the maps have been lost!
If there's a leak, the pipes have to be found somehow!...

It's here somewhere!

HOUSE PIPES

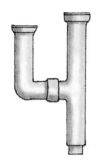 

Most water pipes in a house or school are made of...

PLASTIC or **COPPER**
(for cold water and waste)   (for hot water)

Water pipes used to be made of lead. Then it was found that lead pipes can cause lead poisoning.
This damages the brain!
It's thought that some Roman emperors went mad because they drank water from lead pipes!..

OW!

THUMP!

It's my turn!

Oooh!

Why are we doing this?

Because we're mad!

$$\frac{4\pi^2 \theta}{\lambda^2 l} \gg g!$$

LEAD-FREE WATER

PROFESSOR NOAH LOTT

Some old houses still have lead pipes. If the water stays in the pipes for long enough, it can wear away the lead. Then the lead gets into the water and can cause poisoning.

If you are in a house with lead pipes, you should run the water for a few minutes before you drink any. This runs off the poisoned water before the fresh water arrives at the tap.

WOTTA LOTTA HOTTA BATHS

The Romans didn't have soap, but they liked to keep clean. They invented the

ROMAN BATHS

like this one in the city of Bath in England...

ROMAN NO-SOAP FACT

The Romans used to put olive oil on their skins. Then they scraped it off, together with the dirt, with a flat knife.

Romans often bathed together in places similar to swimming pools.

CLEOPATRA

Cleopatra was a queen of ancient Egypt. It's said that she used to bathe in asses' milk!
She thought that it was good for her skin.

200 PINTS TODAY

WOTTA LOTTA HOTTA BATHS

MUD BATHS

Some people think that mud baths are good for the skin.
BUT...you'd better find out what your parents think before you try one!

SAUNAS

Hot steam softens the skin and makes you sweat. The sweat pushes dirt out of your skin.
Saunas or Steam-baths are very popular in some countries. People sit around in steamy rooms and sweat a lot!

JACUZZIS

A jacuzzi is a modern sort of bath which uses jets of air and water to massage the skin. This helps the blood in the skin to flow more easily, making the jacuzzi user feel more healthy!

BUBBLE BATHS

Bubble baths are great fun. BUT...if everybody used them, the sewage treatment plants would be overloaded with soap suds. Then the rivers would become polluted. Too much soap can be bad for your health!

SILLY SOAP STORIES

There's more to know about soap than how nice it smells and how it cleans your hands.
For example...

SOAP MAKES WATER WETTER!

If you soak some cloth in tap water, you'll see lots of little air-bubbles in it. If you soak another piece of the same cloth in water with soap-powder in it, there will be fewer bubbles in the cloth. That means that the soapy water gets to more of the cloth, making it cleaner and wetter!

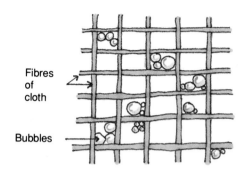

Fibres of cloth

Bubbles

CLOTH IN TAP WATER

CLOTH IN SOAPY WATER

Day dreaming

SOAP OPERAS!

Soap operas aren't about who does the washing up.
At one time, drama series on commercial radio and television were paid for by soap makers. They did this so that they could advertise their products during the commercial breaks.
So...the shows became known as 'Soap Operas' or 'SOAPS'!

SILLY SOAP STORIES

HOW TO MAKE GIANT BUBBLES

It's easy to buy a buy a bubble maker like this from a shop.
BUT...if you want to make huge bubbles, you've got to think BIG!

1. Find a wire clothes hanger.

2. Bend it into shape.

3. Put 500cc of washing-up liquid into a washing-up bowl and fill the bowl with water.

4. Add 200cc of glycerine from a chemist's shop. This makes the bubbles last longer.

5. Scoop all the foamy bubbles from the surface. Then use your giant bubble maker like this...

Dip it in.

Catch a flat bubble.

Slowly move it up and down.

Try to bounce smaller bubbles on your giant bubble.

SHAVING

When you grow up there are even more things to do in the bathroom. Shaving for example.

Most adults shave, even people with beards! Most women don't like to admit that they shave. They think it's not feminine to have body-hair.

Ask your mum if she shaves and see what she says. Try not to laugh too much!

Beards have to be cleaned as well. They can become full of bacteria from food that falls on them!

If an average man never shaved, he'd have a beard eight metres long by the time he was sixty-five years old!

Tea

Biscuits

Apple Pie

Porridge

Fried egg

Haggis

Look out for bearded men and try to spot what they've had for lunch!

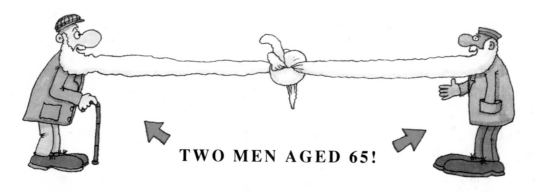

TWO MEN AGED 65!

30

BATH TIME

Shaving takes up about fifteen minutes a day. Over a number of years, that adds up to a lot of time. The two men on page 30 have each saved about six months!

Baths and showers take up about eighteen months of an average life!

Going to the toilet takes up about six months of an average life. Think what it would be like if you could do it all at once!

All that time spent in the bathroom adds up to about two years of an average life. Don't waste it!
You could learn to play the piano in that time if you had a big enough bathroom!

You could get to know all sorts of amazing things. You should always have a book handy in the bathroom. A concise encyclopaedia is a good idea so that you can read little bits at a time!

Now that you've read this book...

LEAVE IT IN THE BATHROOM!

Let other people read it too!

BUT...

Don't let them read it

IN THE SHOWER!..

INDEX